MONSTER GOOSE

MONSTER GOOSE

BY Judy Sierra

ILLUSTRATED BY Jack E. Davis

VOYAGER BOOKS   HARCOURT, INC.   ORLANDO AUSTIN NEW YORK SAN DIEGO TORONTO LONDON

www.HarcourtBooks.com

First Voyager Books edition 2005
Voyager Books is a trademark of Harcourt, Inc., registered in the United States of America and/or other jurisdictions.

The Library of Congress has cataloged the hardcover edition as follows:
Sierra, Judy.
Monster Goose/written by Judy Sierra; illustrated by Jack E. Davis.
p.   cm.
Summary: A collection of twenty-five nursery rhymes, rewritten to feature vampires,
ghouls, mummies, the Loch Ness monster, and other fearsome creatures.
1. Monsters—Juvenile poetry.   2. Children's poetry, American.   3. Nursery rhymes—Adaptations.
[1. Nursery rhymes.   2. Monsters—Poetry.   3. American poetry.]
I. Davis, Jack E., ill.   II. Title.
PS3569.I39M66   2001
811'.54—dc21   00-8808
ISBN 0-15-202034-9
ISBN 0-15-205417-0 pb

C E G H F D

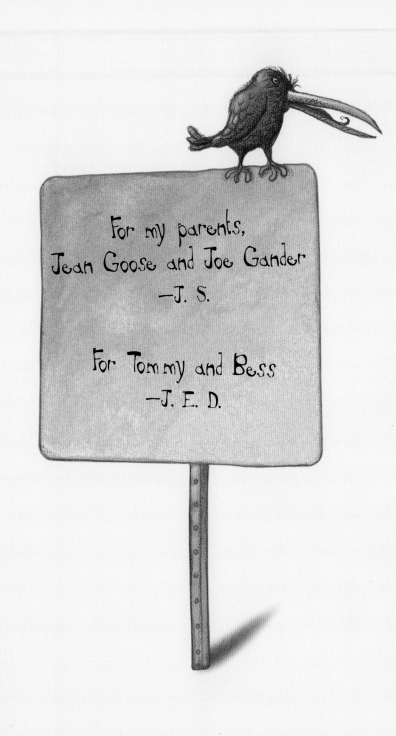

For my parents,
Jean Goose and Joe Gander
—J. S.

For Tommy and Bess
—J. E. D.

Old Monster Goose

Old Monster Goose,
When conditions did suit her,
Pecked out these rhymes
On her laptop computer.

Mary Had a Vampire Bat

Mary had a vampire bat.
His fur was black as night.
He followed her to school one day
And promised not to bite.
She brought him out for show-and-tell;
The teacher screamed and ran.
And school was canceled for a week,
Just as Mary planned.

Corpus McCool

Corpus McCool, the clumsy old ghoul,
Was interred near the gardens at Kew.
He lost his head in the cabbage bed,
And it later appeared in a stew.

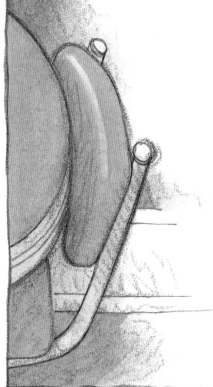

Little Miss Mummy

Little Miss Mummy
Lay on her tummy
Smoking a big cigar.
A very large spider
Resided inside her.
(She kept all her guts in a jar.)

Humpty Dumpty

Humpty Dumpty swam in the sea.
Humpty's sunscreen was SPF-3.
Because he was so lightly oiled,
Dear Humpty ended up hard-boiled.

Pirate Pete

Pirate Pete and Pete's pet shark
Prowl the ocean after dark.
Sailing north and sailing south,
The shark up front with open mouth,
Guided by electric eels,
They search for unsuspecting meals.
So when you take a midnight dip,
Please keep an eye out for Pete's ship.

Rub-a-Dub-Dub

Rub-a-dub-dub,
Three fish in a tub.
And what do you think they do?
Because they're piranhas
With very poor manners,
They hide and wait for you.

PLEASE,
NO
AUTOGRAPHS.

Jill and Jacques

Jill and Jacques
Went to the loch
To fetch a pail of water.
Jill took a swim.
Events turned grim.
The famous monster caught her.

There Was an Old Zombie

There was an old zombie who lived
   in a shoe.
She had so many maggots, she didn't
   know what to do.
So she soaked them in soapsuds and
   painted them green.
She'll be giving them out next
   Halloween.

Cannibal Horner

Cannibal Horner
Sat in the corner
Eating a people potpie.
He bit his own thumb
And cried, "Oh, yum, yum,
A tasty young morsel am I!"

Pussycat, Pussycat

Pussycat, pussycat, where have you been?
—I've been to London to torment
   the queen.
Mean little pussycat, what did you there?
—I put a wee mouse in her long
   underwear.

Weird Mother Hubbard

Weird Mother Hubbard went down to
    the graveyard
To fetch her poor doggy a bone.
But that bone was the toe of Skeleton Joe.
When she took it, Joe followed her home.

She went to the tailor's
To buy Joe a coat,
But when she came back
He was shaving the goat.

She went to the hatter's
To buy Joe a hat,
But when she came back
He was painting the cat.

She went to the baker's
To buy Joe some bread,
But when she came back
He was juggling his head.

The dog said politely,
"This guest has to go."
So Weird Mother Hubbard said,
"TAKE BACK YOUR TOE!"

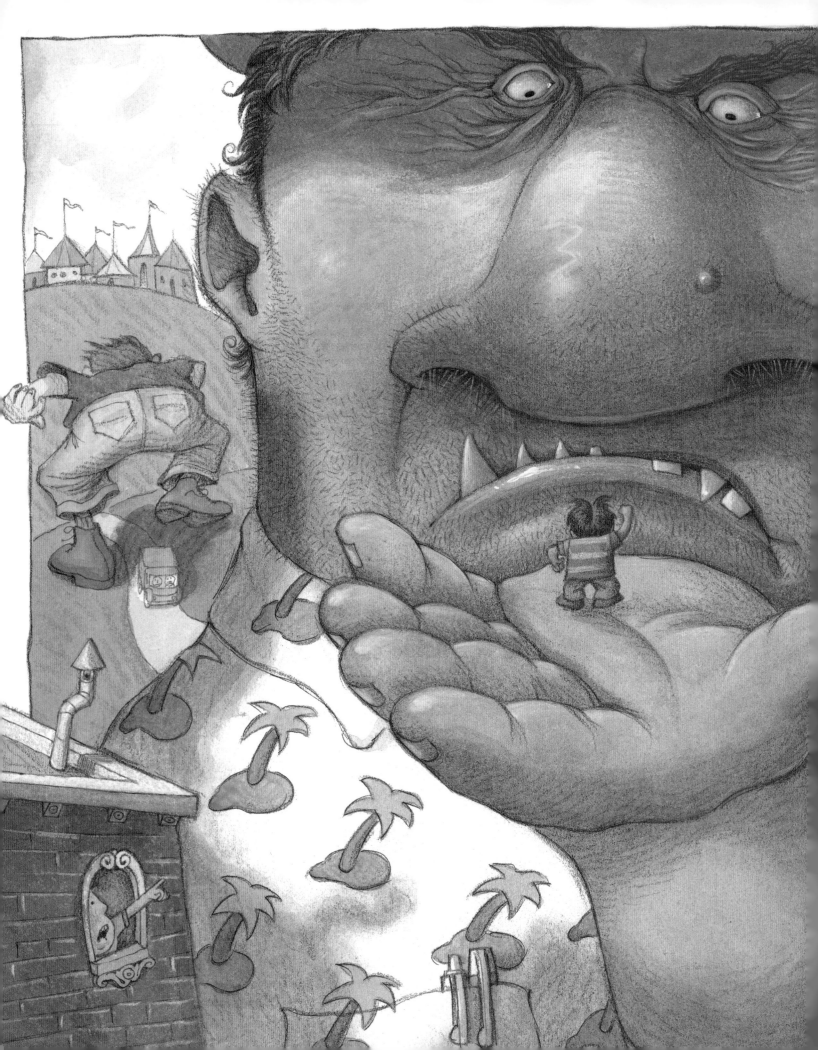

Billy Bryant

Billy Bryant met a giant
Going to the fair.
The giant growled at Billy Bryant,
"Would you like a scare?"
Said Billy Bryant to the giant,
"That would not be fair.
The last three giants that *I* scared
Are in intensive care."

Jack Sprat

Jack Sprat
Ate some fat
And drank some gasoline.
He lit his pipe
And in one swipe
Invented Lean Cuisine.

Hush, Little Monster

Hush, little monster, don't you whine,
Papa's gonna give you to Frankenstein.
If you and Frank can't get along,
Papa's gonna send you to old King Kong.
If you don't like that big gorilla,
You might prefer his friend Godzilla.
If giant lizards make you scared,
Maybe you'll be happy with a grizzly bear.
If life in a bear cave isn't fun,
Why not visit an alien?
If flying through space upsets
    your tummy,
Just come on home to your pappy
    and your mummy.

Slithery, Dithery, Dock

Slithery, dithery, dock,

The snake slid up the clock.

She soon grew bored

And bit the cord.

It gave her quite a shock.

The snake began to quake.

The clock began to rock.

At half past four

They struck the floor.

Smashery, squashery, dock!

There Is a Hungry Boggart

There is a hungry boggart
Living somewhere near my bed.
He gobbled up the sheets
And munched the pillow 'neath my head.
He nibbled my pajamas,
And he swallowed all my toys.
I'm really quite relieved
He has an allergy to boys.

Young King Cole

Young King Cole was a terrible troll:
He washed his feet in the toilet bowl,
Brushed his teeth with turpentine,
And combed his hair with a porcupine.

Mistress Mary

Mistress Mary. Scary? Very!
Her garden is not ordinary:
Her green beans are mean,
    and her chives carry knives.
Her catnip just caught a canary.
A killer potato ate all her tomatoes,
And now he is looking for Mary.

Sing a Song of Sea Slime

Sing a song of sea slime, sewer gas,
   and sludge.
Four and twenty wharf rats dipped in
   mocha fudge.
When the dish was served, it scampered
   out the door.
"Dessert has fled," the poor king said.
   "I guess I'll lick the floor."

The Itsy-Bitsy Spider

The itsy-bitsy spider
Climbed up the warthog's snout.
The warthog grabbed a hankie
And tried to blow it out.
The little bloke was blasted
All the way to Spain,
So the itsy-bitsy spider
Did not go there again.

Werewolf Bo-Creep

Werewolf Bo-Creep has lost his sheep
And doesn't know where to find them.
But they're vampire sheep,
And right now as he sleeps,
They're sneaking up behind him.

Twinkle, Twinkle, Little Slug

Twinkle, twinkle, little slug,
Crawling on my bedroom rug.
In my sister's sock you go.
Wrap yourself around her toe.
Won't my sister love you so?
Twinkle, twinkle, little slug,
Crawling on my bedroom rug.

The Mungery Man

The mungery man and his dangery dog
Once sat on the banks of a blueberry bog,
Munching flat former frogs and mementos
 of mice,
Served up on the peel of an eel, over ice.
They sang, "Wabazoo! Such a feast for
 us two!"
As they slowly dissolved into blueberry goo.

The illustrations in this book were done in acrylics and colored pencil on watercolor paper.

The text type was set in Bernhard Gothic Medium.

Color separations by Bright Arts Ltd., Hong Kong

Printed and bound by Tien Wah Press, Singapore

Production supervision by Pascha Gerlinger

Designed by Judythe Sieck